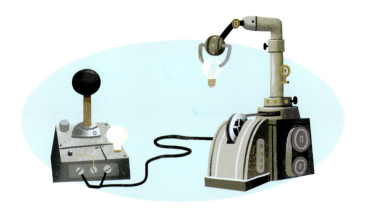

Learning to Read, Step by Step!

Ready to Read Preschool–Kindergarten
• big type and easy words • rhyme and rhythm • picture clues
For children who know the alphabet and are eager to begin reading.

Reading with Help Preschool–Grade 1
• basic vocabulary • short sentences • simple stories
For children who recognize familiar words and sound out new words with help.

Reading on Your Own Grades 1–3
• engaging characters • easy-to-follow plots • popular topics
For children who are ready to read on their own.

Reading Paragraphs Grades 2–3
• challenging vocabulary • short paragraphs • exciting stories
For newly independent readers who read simple sentences with confidence.

Ready for Chapters Grades 2–4
• chapters • longer paragraphs • full-color art
For children who want to take the plunge into chapter books but still like colorful pictures.

STEP INTO READING® is designed to give every child a successful reading experience. The grade levels are only guides; children will progress through the steps at their own speed, developing confidence in their reading.

Remember, a lifetime love of reading starts with a single step!

To Andrea Beaty, who is always asking "What if . . . ?" and inspiring kids to do the same —E.S.P.

Dad, I think you would like this book. —M.S.

Acknowledgments: The author and editor gratefully acknowledge the help of Sharon Klotz, Head of Invention Education, and the library staff at the Lemelson Center for the Study of Invention and Innovation, Smithsonian Institution, National Museum of American History. Thank you very much!

Text copyright © 2020 by Erica S. Perl
Cover art and interior illustrations copyright © 2020 by Michael Slack

All rights reserved. Published in the United States by Random House Children's Books, a division of Penguin Random House LLC, New York.

Step into Reading, Random House, and the Random House colophon are registered trademarks of Penguin Random House LLC.

Photograph credits: Cover, pp. 8 (top and bottom), 9, 45 (bottom right): courtesy of Library of Congress; title page, p. 15 (bottom): courtesy of Param Jaggi; p. 4 (left): Classroom Camera (Cascade Canyon School), Image DSC03538/Flickr Creative Commons; p. 4 (right): Arthur Tilley/Getty Images; p. 5: Shutterstock; pp. 10, 12: courtesy of 3M; p. 13: Signe Dons/Wikimedia Commons; p. 16 (top): Angela Weiss/Stringer/Getty Images; p. 16 (bottom): Uncharted Play; p. 17: picture alliance/Getty Images; p. 18: Universal Images Group/Getty Images; p. 19: courtesy of The New York Public Library; pp. 23 (top left and top right), 33 (bottom): Unknown/Wikimedia Commons; p. 23 (middle right): Heritage Images/Getty Images; p. 23 (bottom left): Matthew Yohe/Wikimedia Commons; p. 23 (bottom right): Interim Archives/Getty Images; p. 25 (top): Alex Handy/Douglas Engelbart/Wikimedia Commons; p. 25 (middle): SRI International/Wikimedia Commons; p. 25 (bottom): Juan Sebastian Torres/Flickr Creative Commons; p. 29: courtesy of Kohler Co.; p. 32: Luca/Wikimedia Commons; p. 33 (top): Classic Image/Alamy Stock Photo; p. 34 (top): Office of Naval Research/Flickr Creative Commons; p. 34 (bottom): INTERFOTO/Alamy Stock Photo; pp. 35 (top), 36, 40: Bettmann/Getty Images; p. 35 (bottom): Science History Institute/Wikimedia Commons; p. 41: John Tamblyn/courtesy of Rachel Zimmerman; p. 45 (top left): restored by Adam Cuerden/Tuskegee University Archives/Museum/Wikimedia Commons; p. 45 (top right): courtesy of Morehead State Public Radio, WMKY-FM; p. 45 (bottom left): Employee(s) of MGM/Wikimedia Commons

Visit us on the Web!
StepIntoReading.com
rhcbooks.com

Educators and librarians, for a variety of teaching tools, visit us at RHTeachersLibrarians.com

Library of Congress Cataloging-in-Publication Data.
Names: Perl, Erica S., author. | Slack, Michael H., illustrator.
Title: Truth or lie : inventors! / by Erica S. Perl ; illustrations by Michael Slack.
Description: New York : Random House Children's Books, 2020. | Series: Step into reading. Step 3 | Audience: Ages 5–8 | Audience: Grades 2–3 |
Summary: "A book made up of 75% truths and 25% lies, challenging kids to spot what is false in this fun reader about inventors" —Provided by publisher.
Identifiers: LCCN 2019050176 (print) | LCCN 2019050177 (ebook) |
ISBN 978-1-9848-9521-9 (paperback) | ISBN 978-1-9848-9522-6 (library binding) |
ISBN 978-1-9848-9523-3 (ebook)
Subjects: LCSH: Inventors—Miscellanea—Juvenile literature. | Inventions—Miscellanea—Juvenile literature.
Classification: LCC T48 .P45 2020 (print) | LCC T48 (ebook) | DDC 600—dc23

MANUFACTURED IN CHINA

10 9 8 7 6 5 4 3 2

Random House Children's Books supports the First Amendment and celebrates the right to read.

A HISTORY READER

TRUTH or LIE
INVENTORS!

by Erica S. Perl
illustrations by Michael Slack

Random House 🏠 New York

Hi! It's me!
The TRUTH SLEUTH.
Just *popping* in to say
that bubble gum,
bubble wrap,
and bubble tea
were all invented by inventors.

It's TRUE!

But I smell a LIE nearby.

Let's play TRUTH OR LIE and find it!

When you turn the page,

you'll see four statements . . .

BUT only three are TRUE.

An inventor also invented speech bubbles, like this one.

Let's go! Which one is a LIE?

1. The first self-propelled airplane stayed in the air for twelve minutes.

2. The first automobile had only three wheels.

3. The first steam train was too heavy for its track.

4. The first pedal-powered bicycle had a huge front wheel and a tiny rear wheel.

Did you guess that the lie is #1? Right!

The first self-propelled airplane stayed in the air for twelve minutes. [LIE]

Actually, it stayed in the air for just twelve *seconds*. But the Wright brothers, who invented this plane, did not give up.

Orville and Wilbur Wrig

Being an inventor means trying different options while perfecting an invention. Within two years, they built a plane that could fly for about forty minutes.

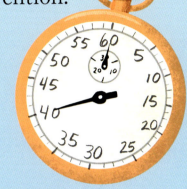

Hmm . . . I'm stuck!
Do you see a LIE here?

1. Spencer Silver invented a strange glue that didn't stay stuck.

2. Silver met Arthur Fry while stuck in an elevator.

3. Fry thought up an idea for Silver's strange glue.

4. Together, Silver and Fry created a household item.

The lie is #2.

Silver met Arthur Fry while stuck in an elevator. ~~LIE~~

Silver and Fry were scientists who met at their workplace. Fry, who sang in a choir, complained that his bookmarks fell out of his hymn books.

He decided to try
Silver's strange glue
to help paper stick
to his books
without damaging them.
Eureka! Silver and Fry
invented Post-it Notes.

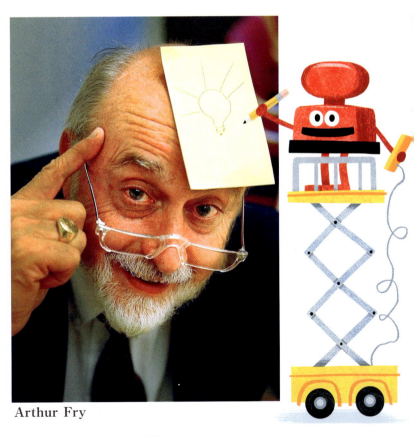

Arthur Fry

I spy another lie nearby. Can you find a LIE here?

1. Inventors created a light that's powered by playing soccer.

2. Inventors developed a straw that filters unclean water as you drink.

3. An inventor made a weather machine that can make it stop raining.

4. An inventor came up with a device that uses pond scum to help a car create less pollution.

Did you guess #3?

An inventor made a weather machine that can make it stop raining. LIE

So far, no invention can control the weather. But some inventions can help our planet. Playing with the Soccket soccer ball creates clean energy and turns the ball into a light.

Jessica Matthews

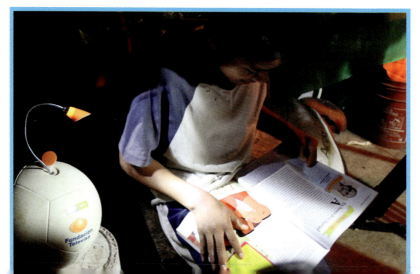

LifeStraw provides access to clean drinking water.

And if you smell something swampy, look around.
The Algae Mobile, invented by Param Jaggi, might be nearby!

Oh, me, oh, my! Another LIE?

1. Candido Jacuzzi invented the whirlpool bathtub that bears his name.

2. The word "sandwich" was named after John Montagu, the 4th Earl of Sandwich, who enjoyed meals between two slices of bread.

3. The leotard was named after Jules Léotard,
   who proudly wore it
   on his flying trapeze.

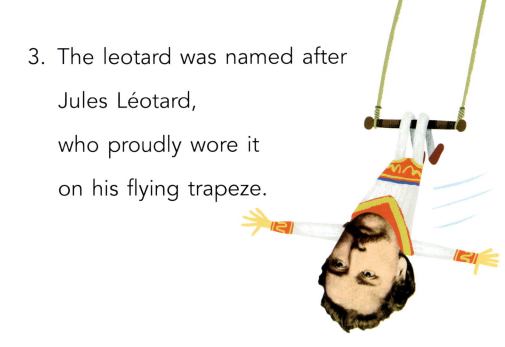

4. Sarah Suspenders got tired
   of her husband's pants falling down,
   and she used their last name
   for her invention.

It's #4!

Sarah Suspenders got tired of her husband's pants falling down, and she used their last name for her invention. LIE

Actually, suspenders were first manufactured by Albert Thurston.

But many inventions were named after their inventors. The bowler hat, the diesel engine, and the Ferris wheel are all named for their inventors.

Can you figure out
which one is the LIE?

1. Charles Babbage and Ada Lovelace came up with the first programmable computing machine.
2. Alan Turing invented the concept of software— the programs that can make a computer do amazing things.
3. Steve Jobs invented the computer mouse.
4. Grace Hopper invented the compiler, which translates instructions into computer codes.

The lie is #3!

Steve Jobs invented the computer mouse. LIE

Steve Jobs and his team at Apple were modern computing pioneers. They invented the Macintosh computer, iPod, iPad, and iPhone.

However, the mouse was invented by another computer scientist, Douglas Engelbart. The device got its name because it was tiny and had a long, tail-like cord.

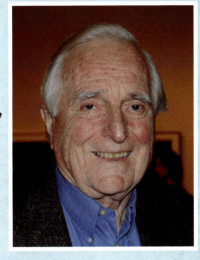

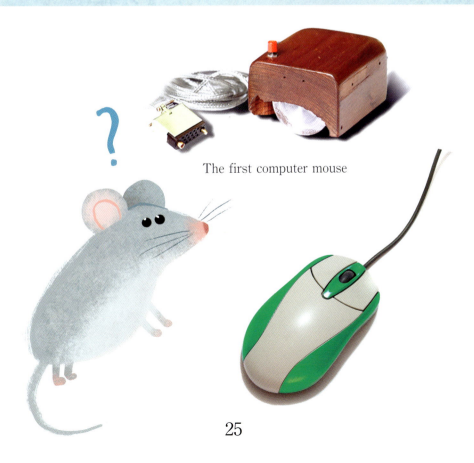

The first computer mouse

Okay, smarty-pants!

See if you can find another LIE.

1. Smartphones have been invented.

2. Smart octopuses have been invented.

3. Smart refrigerators have been invented.

4. Smart toilets have been invented.

Believe it or not, the lie is #2!

Smart octopuses have been invented.

It's true that some animals are surprisingly smart. But no inventor can take credit for an animal's natural intelligence. Inventors do deserve credit for artificial intelligence, or "AI." Products with AI have been programmed to do tasks that usually require a human.

In response to voice commands,
smart toilets can
warm the seat,
adjust the lighting,
play music,
and, of course, flush.

Read all about it!

There's another LIE to find!

1. The first alphabet had 226 letters.

2. The first books were carved into clay and handwritten on scrolls.

3. The first mechanical printing press was based on a fruit press.

4. The first newspaper was published in Germany in 1605.

The lie is #1!

The first alphabet had 226 letters.

The first alphabet had just 22 letters. It was created by the Phoenicians between 1700 and 1500 BCE.

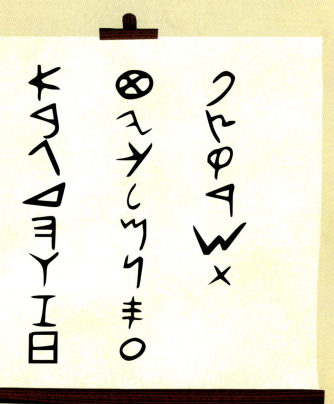

Over 2,500 years later, Chinese inventor Bi Sheng invented movable type: carved clay blocks that could print over and over. About 400 years later, German inventor Johannes Gutenberg created the first mechanical printing press.

Surprise! Let's find another LIE.

1. NASA engineer Lonnie Johnson was working on a new kind of heat pump when he invented the Super Soaker toy.

2. Ruth Wakefield made an ingredient substitution that led to the invention of a popular cookie.

3. Frank Epperson didn't like hamburgers,

   so he invented the hot dog.

4. Chemist Stephanie Kwolek was trying to improve car tires when she invented Kevlar, the material used for bulletproof vests.

It's #3!

Frank Epperson didn't like hamburgers, so he invented the hot dog. LIE

Actually, Frank Epperson invented the Popsicle, not the hot dog!

On a chilly evening,
eleven-year-old Frank left
a cup of soda outside
with a wooden stirrer in it.
The next morning,
he found a new frozen treat.
Like the Popsicle,
many inventions
have come about
accidentally.

There's a LIE here. No kidding!

1. When Rachel Zimmerman
   was twelve years old,
   she invented a device
   so non-speaking people
   could communicate using
   a touch pad.
2. When Louis Braille was
   fifteen years old,
   he invented Braille,
   a system of raised dots that
   blind people can read.
3. In eighth grade,
   Trisha Prabhu
   was motivated to invent
   an anti-bullying app.

4. Sixteen-year-old gymnast George Nissen bounced to fame by inventing the pogo stick.

The one that doesn't fly is #4!

Sixteen-year-old gymnast George Nissen bounced to fame by inventing the pogo stick. LIE

George Nissen didn't invent the pogo stick.
But he did invent the trampoline!

Many of the world's greatest
inventions were created by kids.
Some, like Louis Braille,
invented things they needed.
(Louis Braille was blind.)
Some, like Rachel Zimmerman,
got their start
at school science fairs.
Maybe you'll be
the next great inventor!

Rachel Zimmerman

So many LIES! And you need to find one more.

1. George Washington Carver invented over three hundred uses for the peanut.

2. Thomas Edison invented the joystick.

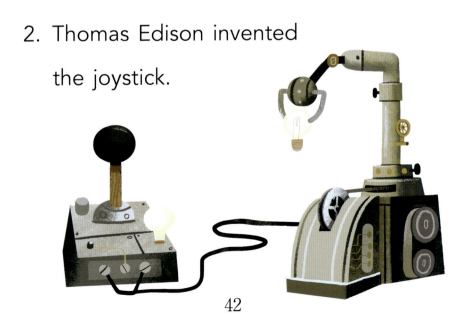

3. Margaret Knight invented a machine that manufactured flat-bottomed grocery bags.

4. Actress Hedy Lamarr was honored by the National Inventors Hall of Fame for her inventions involving wireless communication.

I feel like we are drifting apart.

Don't worry. We're wireless.

Did you guess #2?

Thomas Edison invented the joystick.

Thomas Edison developed
over a thousand inventions,
but the joystick
was not one of them.
Edison was honored by the
National Inventors Hall of Fame,
along with George Washington Carver,
Hedy Lamarr, Margaret Knight,
and many other pioneering inventors.

George Washington Carver

Margaret Knight

Hedy Lamarr

Thomas Edison

Do you want to be an inventor?
Here's what to do:
Be curious about
how things work.
Try things many times
and many ways.
And never give up!

You did it!
You are officially a
TRUTH SLEUTH like me.
Keep up the good work!

- Read with an eye for TRUTH and a nose for LIES.
- Share what you know *and* how you figured out it was TRUE.
- Ask your parents, guardian, teacher, or librarian to help you find the best books and most reliable websites.
- Play TRUTH OR LIE with your friends and family.

Want to Learn More FACTS About Inventors?

Books to read:

African American Inventors by Stephen Currie (Lucent Books, 2010)

Calling All Minds: How to Think and Create Like an Inventor by Temple Grandin (Penguin, 2018)

Girls Think of Everything: Stories of Ingenious Inventions by Women by Catherine Thimmesh, illustrated by Melissa Sweet (Houghton Mifflin Harcourt, 2018)

1,000 Inventions and Discoveries by Roger Bridgman (DK, 2014)

So You Want to Be an Inventor? by Judith St. George and David Small (Philomel Books, 2002)

What a Great Idea! Inventions That Changed the World by Stephen M. Tomecek, illustrated by Dan Stuckenschneider (Scholastic, 2003)

Websites to check out:

britannica.com/topic/inventor

destinationimagination.org

invent.org

invention.si.edu/node/11457/p/465-current-members